BELOVED INFIDEL

ALSO BY DEAN YOUNG

BELOVED INFIDEL

Poems

Dean Young

Hollyridge Press
Venice, California

Hollyridge Press
P.O. Box 2872
Venice, California 90294

Cover Design by Ian Randall Wilson / Dean Young
Cover Art:
"Nipigon Window" ©Frank J. Hutton, 2003. All Rights Reserved.
"Praying Mantis" by Annette DeGiovine Oliveira
Dendrite Rendering courtesy of Dr. Frederic Libersat
Zlotowski Center for Neuroscience, Ben Gurion University
Author photo by P. James Fotos
Manufactured in the United States of America by Lightning Source

Publisher's Cataloging-in-Publication
(Provided by Cassidy Cataloguing Services)

Young, Dean, 1955-

Beloved infidel : poems / Dean Young. -- Venice, Calif. :
Hollyridge Press, 2004.

p. ; cm.

Reprint. Originally published: Hanover, NH : University
Press of New England, 1992.
ISBN: 0-9676003-9-1

I. Title.

PS3575.O782 B45 2004   2004101251
811/.54--dc22   0406

11 10 09 08 07 06 05 04   10 9 8 7 6 5 4 3 2 1

for CLAUDIA YOUNG and again for NEAL

Content is a glimpse. —Willem de Kooning

Acknowledgments

Thanks to the editors of the following magazines in which some of these poems first appeared: *Antioch Review, Black Warrior Review, Crazyhorse, Denver Quarterly, Gettysburg Review, Indiana Review, Ironwood, Poetry East, Poetry Northwest, New American Writing, North American Review, Sulfur* and *Threepenny Review*. "Bouquet on the Third Day" and "The Afterlife" first appeared in *Ploughshares*; "Elegy for My Cat" and "Transubstantiation" first appeared in *The Ohio Review*. "Storms" and "Other Obit" were included in *New American Poets of the 90's*. "The Business of Love is Cruelty" also appeared in *Best American Poetry, 1993*.

Thanks to these musicians whose work has been inspiring: Van Morrison, Keith Jarrett, David Sylvian, David Torn, Kazumi Watanabe, and Bill Frisell. Gratitude is due the following for assistance during the writing of these poems: National Endowment for the Arts; Fine Arts Work Center, Provincetown; Stanford University; Indiana University; University of Wisconsin; Loyola University of Chicago; and University Press Books, Berkeley.

Thanks to these friends and teachers for their help and suggestions: Kevin Stein, Roger Mitchell, Lynda Hull, Clint McCown, Tom Rea, Jim Harris, W.S. DiPiero, Ron Wallace, Lorrie Moore, Keith Ratzlaff, Alan Mahrenholz, Jim Harms, Dale Kushner, David Michael Kaplan, David Rivard. Special thanks to Tony Hoagland and David Wojahn.

Contents

4

1

DRAMA IN LAST ACTS

Throughout the days of summer will be portrayed
by tiers of bells wheeled across the stage.
From the beginning the intensity
will be rivaled only by bulbs slapped
and burning brightly before burning out.
Plucked chickens lowered on ropes
will be understood as meaning disaster
just as the old man laboring over the message
will be understood as a king laboring over a message.
I can see I'm going to have to start over.
I don't know which of Melissa's cast parties
was the best, the one with the mannequins
or the one with the chickens on ropes
or the one where we arrived just as the cops
cruised up and we walked past, flimsy
with our contraband, our faces hot
beneath the masks. You won't believe
what I went through to get her back.
All of you, over there!
We put right angles of tape on the stage,
color-coded. Throughout the summer they love each other.
She was brokenhearted about the binoculars.
The going-to-hell scene would be done with saxophones,
given the budget limitations.
What else could all the green velvet mean
and that couch with the lion's paws?
Such simple things: glass, rope,
left to right. Just tell me where I stand.
We sat not talking, the list of numbers between us.
I kept waiting for the fierce dogs to come from the fog
or *I love you I love you I love you.*

We built the fire carefully but were completely
unprepared for the red triangle. Then I lost her
in the smoke. Again. Then I lost her.
Try it without the sword. I lost her.
No starting over now.
Your seat is B-3. Your seat is DD-9.
Everyone agrees that the pomegranate
makes all the difference, and worse, on the sixth night,
Bill forgot and only a banana could be quickly found.
Imagine a whip instead of the binoculars
or a lily or a small girl with an oar.
They sat not looking at each other.
Already trees losing leaves.
Now what, she cried but it was more a projection
of her crying, you could see the exit lights
through her forehead. Lost. And in desire
to sing like a tree losing its leaves.
Is this how it ends? she asks, bunching up
her coat. I held the little flashlight
disguised as a candle that made me feel holy
just as the white gloves made me feel
invulnerable and nearly vanished.

THE AFTERLIFE

Four A.M. and the trees in their nocturnal turns
seem free from our ideas of what trees should be
like the moment in a dance you let your partner go
and suddenly she's loose fire and unapproachable.
Yesterday I saw L again, by a case of kiwis
and she seemed wrongly tall as if wearing cothurni.
Would it be better never to see her at all?
In Jim's poem about death, shirts pile on a chair.
I imagine them folded, the way shirts are,
arms behind the back, then boxed in mothballs
and marked with Magic Marker, Jim's Shirts.
Probably what would really happen
is his wife might save a few to hang among her own.
Even that off-the-shoulder thing of hers
commingled with grief, overlapping ghosts.
The rest she'd give away, maybe dump
in a Salvation Army bin in some parking lot
or just drop off in People's Park. It scares me
to think of that guy with sores on his face
trying on the parrot shirt. It scares me
how well it fits. Maybe if I just walked up to her
and said, Enough. Maybe she still has my blue belt.
Outside, the rain riffs off the shingles, wind
mews down the exhaust tube of my heater.
On the isinglass flames rush in smudges
like lovers who must pass through each other
as punishment for too much lust and feeding.

BELOVED INFIDEL

There was no end to it. Desire.
It took moments, monstrous moments. Desire.
He made a sandwich and put on piano music.
She wanted him to say what he meant to say
not what he said he said. He sliced it in half.
There were preparatory warnings
in the form of insects on the windowsill,
desiccated in the globular bellies
of the overhead lights. Desire and fear of desire.
That dust stirred up. The toothpicks shoved in
and something like flames above their heads
in versions of holiness, of yearning in flames
and those folded white napkins.
I wish you'd just say yes, just stroke
my hand with yours. They were trying
to have lunch on the lawn. Simply, someone said,
simply tell us when you began to feel like this.
Think of a place, the rooms by the water,
sun mizzling at the window, the usual
rubble, the dog locked out, braying.
I didn't know how alone I was
until they brought out more chairs.
Now where are you? I was feeding the birds
and it was terrifying as if for a second
live coals were put in my mouth
as in truth I once axed a beehive
and they flew in me, in my mouth. swarming.
Oh fear, oh my kingdom, I am afraid
of even birds, of all they've come to mean
of loss, their pink retreating feet. Afraid
of fog, gentle fog, afraid of your face
that day drunkenly I drug in the boat

on its mooring rope and you refused to enter.
Look, I'm trying. First we were on a beach
then in a house interspersed with memories.
Forget the other him and her. First we were on a beach
and I kept trying to say what I wanted.
In the garden someone had plucked the petals
from the flowers, carefully and with conviction.

WHAT DOES US IN

I can live without you nearly. Some days
I need only erase and erase until it's not
a cigar I smoke in the wedding photos where
I first saw you in the billiard room,
all the tables retired under velvet shrouds.
You're dancing alone with three champagne
glasses also empty. But now amid the larval
rubbings I hold only a gritty wing to my mouth,
swaddled entirely in smoke. Smoke
I can live with. It is, after all, what
we're made of, our gowns and wishes
and recriminations. But we must not
be afraid, my countrymen. All evening I
bend the wire I find coming home from work.
Mostly snips. Mostly snips. Horse with wings,
man with three arms, man with none. It goes on
and on and then it stops. That electric under-hum. That swabbing
and subtle bleating, the terrible dents in the pillows.
And death-heads I can live with
like what glowed that night as my friends spoke
of the fragile pregnancy between them,
the caulk gun on the back sill,
smooth muscle relaxers racing her heart.
So as they spoke the death-heads shone
beneath their skins like a grin sometimes
tics my face when I lie. Almost everyone I know
is held together with tape and making an F
then a T sound like a match fizzling out.
Above the deli boxes and delft plates,
the last of the lemon sherbet melting.
There and there and nothing could dispel it,
not the impersonations of horn and lute.

Not the yellow marker or the blue, not
lashing the dog with the chthonic roses.
My heart hurts like a revolving tray of sweets.
It was the hats that my mother broke down about.
Not that there were so many of my father's hats,
just that he had worn them, a man who went to work
and came home, liked his meat nearly burnt, liked
gin and bitters and politics. That those hats
would be left, no wonder.

THE BUSINESS OF LOVE IS CRUELTY

It scares me, the genius we have
for hurting one another. I'm seven,
as tall as my mother kneeling and
she's kneeling and somehow I know

exactly how to do it, calmly,
enunciating like a good actor projecting
to the last row, shocking the ones
who've come in late, cowering

out of their coats, sleet still sparking
on their collars, a voice nearly licking
their ears above the swordplay and laments:
I hate you.

Now her hands are rising to her face.
Now the fear done flashing through me,
I wish I could undo it, take it back,
but it's a question of perfection,

carrying it through, climbing the steps
to my room, chosen banishment, where
I'll paint the hair of my model
Bride of Frankenstein purple and pink,

heap of rancor, vivacious hair
that will not die. She's rejected
of course her intended, cathected
the desires of six or seven bodies

onto the wimp Doctor. And Herr Doktor,
what does he want among the burning villages

of his proven theories? Well, he wants
to be a student again, free, drunk,

making the cricket jump, but
his distraught monster's on the rampage
again, lead-footed, weary, a corrosive
and incommunicable need sputtering

his chest, throwing oil like a fouled-up
motor: how many times do you have to die
before you're dead?

COMET

After she left I sat trying to quiet,
the pain still wicking my arm where I caught
the sink as she ironed her silk rose.
Already those moments fixed in their case
with its velvet moment-sized indentations.
Already I remember this summer as the summer
every letter came with news of sick parents.
We'd fall asleep to music, our shadows
abstract, mounting away from the light.
In the house we rented, the portrait
of the nail heiress rots, inept, diseased,
one arm slithering without an elbow
out from a nest of finery. And that morning,
the record low tide, maybe a hundred shoes
in the fat sand, tarred, slugged with mussels.
I can't say it wasn't expected.
Afixing that rose to her throat. Sometimes
I feel a part of myself roam off, as in grief,
I turn from the overladen table, taking one grape,
one mint, avoiding the cousins talking cars.
It would be the summer I waited for her,
sitting on the curb in my best trousers
among the chewings and spits, the drivers
negotiating the turn, the sun picking up
its measuring sticks, the next thing coming.
In the meantime, I might have let a woman cry.
I might have classified all the limps of the world
by cause. Everything through the fire looks
beckoning as dawn, as memories of childhood.
At one edge an X. At the other an X.
It was the summer hundreds gathered at dusk
in parks to see the comet, children crying,

No, I can't. Even through the apparatus,
it was just a gritty streak, a place in the sky
where something had been poorly erased.

SHADES

I'm drinking with Richard who I haven't
seen in years, not since Tuesday night
tae kwon do when we practiced kicking
cigarettes from each other's mouths.

He's telling me about Fern running a hose
from her exhaust and idling to death in a Saab.
Something's funny about his syntax, as if
one unclosed parenthesis traipsed behind

another like that progression of shades
who must be beat back so Odysseus
can find out how to get home.
Of course my friend's lost.

Of course he's trying to forget how once,
after revolving through the store doors,
she spit shoplifted cufflinks into his hand.
Of course the rain hot through the hot clouds

and smoke from his cigarette rises as if
with some intention forever veiled from us,
forever superior, free of our lumpy intervention,
the tonnage of our couplings. What can I say

that isn't a contrivance of keening and
projection? How twice a woman I once loved
told me gently almost politely
sometimes she wishes me dead?

I hadn't suffered but the house is hers.
No more avant-garde guitar, no piss on the seat.

She'd make a few calls and teach Greek bravely
the next weeks but keep coming back

to needing me in our dehiscent and husked world,
half our faces insistent flicker, half
hooded with departure at dusk. Now
I think of us as just two probabilities

undressing in rented rooms by choppy water.
First the door number, then her wardrobe,
finally the bitterness and the pain like
erasing a trapezoid. It's the part of the story

where I always find myself fiddling with matches
or coins. The part where you're supposed to feel
more. The part where the person across from you
lumbers into sobs and you can only reach

for the bill. He thinks of his world now
like a bat's, made entirely of avoided,
ricocheted screams. Well, it's not what
he expected. But what do any of us expect,

coming up to one another with the look
of someone who's carried something a long time
in his mouth: secret or bolt or cherry pit,
a mouthful of water across a desert

to spit out in insult to the body
and the body's thirsts. I'm not sure
why I love that moment in Hell
when Tiresias gripes, *You again*

to Odysseus before he swills goat's blood.
The Greek dead know everything but without
any sense of order, it's all already over,
even the future, even the coming day

when Odysseus drops his oar
far from any sea, but for us—
we bat back and forth, trying to
figure out what happened and happened to us,

weeping and swallowing our weeping,
barely visible even to each other.

BOUQUET ON THE THIRD DAY

The small white roses are the first to bow,
drying closed to withered buds
the way I've seen a girlishness
fold over my mother ordering in restaurants,
finding a seat on the bus. See, see.
The small white roses and freesias
and red berries falling from the rhapsodic stalk.
See what the earth has done.

Now the baby in the front house is up,
I hear her mother's waltzing coo
and the birds on their sweet apexes.
A dog, blocks off, ends its decree
with one high yelp of suffering
the way we're all reduced by suffering
this locked gate, our bowls upset
and clattering in the dust.

Last night on a hill above the city,
my friends and I watched the bridge lit
after twenty burnt-out years, all the bulbs
new. While the mayor threw the switch,
ships passed on the bay like hats
with candles in their brims,
like what they say Van Gogh wore
to paint the Loire at night
and how else approach beauty in its current
except in an outfit of flicker and wax?

In the city another poet died last week
and one version of this elegy goes on
in only waterways: Susquehanna, Amazon,

Danube, San Francisco Bay but how much
can one man take? Brenda remembers
whole poems intact, especially the one
about the falconer she once had her daughter
read aloud. Sunday, hung over. You know
the halt and battle of a child
reading aloud and yes, my friend is crying
so all of us know the soaping power
of tears, their great enzymes, the film
wiped away. the bowing, bowing, the flame
and water and bone, the lid of fog coming down.
There's the soul again making its rough crossing.
There's the soul again with its long retinue.

2

BIOGRAPHY WITH LACK OF SLEEP

Last night the party down the street
quit its shrieks and bellows around three—
there seemed to be no dying out, no
whimper or fight calmed down, just
the peacock Mick Jagger finally
clicked off as if someone had said,
That war's over, lost, the maimed
all decorated and/or dead. Below
my window a couple murmured
in the molasses of their soused
affection. Perhaps she lives downstairs,
the one with the loud answering machine:
Anne, it's 2 o'clock and I'm going swimming.
Anne, I'm sorry about this afternoon.
Husky, their voices, glazed between
insistence and delay, enact
what their bodies will soon enact
as if they could kindle between their legs
some trifling fire from which would rise
a giant butterfly with eyes on its wings
and an appetite solely for nectar.
I remember parties ending like that,
wafting with a drunken girl through
the orchard of my drunken friends
until one night—maybe this happens for all of us—
The truth, I said, turning off the music.
By then she had stopped crying when we fought
as if something had been brought up
from as deep as we'd ever get, exploding
in our thin air, flecking us with prismatic
scales. It was reaching a kind of end
like knowing from here on in you'd have

to get more sleep, put something in the bank
and there's something funny happening
to your knees. Outside, down the block,
the el passes off its interpretation of the sea,
its insistence and delay, its breaking and beckoning,
everything polished, polished and ground to dust.
These days that begin with puffs of dark
still clinging to the doorways and oaks,
it's part of what I think of when I think
of love, like smoke, I thought, watching her
in bed, the languorous inhale and sudden
stabbing out.

PLEASURE

One of those times I knew even then
I couldn't inhabit fully enough.
Lunch late, Duncan and Neal ordering Cobb Salad—
whatever whoever Cobb is—
and how wonderful to order something you've never heard of
even if the ingredients
are right there beside it
in their crisp assertive adjectives.
But what I ordered was corned beef.
Hot.
Our service strange:
our waiter takes our water off as if we've already left
as if to remind us how ephemeral all pleasures are
but then brought us coffee we didn't order
which we take.
Or took.
Time goes by in no time at all, confusing
all my tenses, Duncan's watch on Indiana time
keeps telling us we're late, Neal rattling on
about our chances in Bellingham,
shadows turning long and blue outside,
people in other booths leaning into each other,
feeding each other, inventing new forms
of procreation. In moments like these
the hothouse was invented. The kite.
The sandwich. I might have been lost
in the Delaware of my beloved's hair
as I rowed my heart to the restroom:
a long, odd way: out the restaurant and through
the lobby of a hotel I didn't know was there,
fussed-up with abstract art like sea gulls
thrown donuts in a storm, the concierge

atomizing her approval of where I asked to go,
of what I was about to do, had done, about
that whole arena of the body and its imperatives,
so why must I feel so guilty? Misery, misery
flush the automatic urinals as if I've wandered in
from a slide show of what the junta did
to the hill people. What livid stepparent
steps into my room and finds me with the Sunday-section bra ads?
Atrocities traipse across front pages
but creak creak goes the machinery of my heart
as I return to my table, as I swim back
to happiness, people making decisions solely
based on pleasure even though they choose low-cal,
even as they chew with their mouths open,
telling about the dreadful things their first husbands did,
the thing a sister said that hurt them, the time
they stepped on the urchin snorkeling
and that was the end of Florida.
Oh, it's all mixed up: the past, the present,
pain and pleasure and there's something
inexplicably sweet in my mouth considering
it's just perfectly okay corned beef,
it need not be the best I've ever had
and yes, yes, all over the world people
are suffering the basest sorts of deprivations
but don't we owe this pleasure our commitment,
our awe of this gift god's proffered us
or whatever we've replaced god with?
Creak, creak.
It's why we're given taste buds, so many nerves
in our lips and fingertips, why the piano, the cactus,
why women have clitorises, why and what for
frogs and pepper and the moon and no,
this isn't the light of wisdom,
it's the indirect lighting of joy,
of seduction, little fake candles on our tables

with bulbs shaped like flames and cars shaped
like flames, lovers shaped like flames
and the shoes of lovers.
Outside, above the road, eight-foot lips
declare desires we've just begun to formulate
in the test tubes of our yearning
and outside even further, there's a spot on the overpass
that must have required hanging upside down
to proclaim the beloved's name above the traffic:
spray paint,
only the first letter botched.
I remember being a boy in winter woods,
snow and women's underwear snagged in a tree;
oh, what mystery and a little menace like a good movie.
I thought one day I might be
if not exactly privy to a woman throwing her drawers in a tree
then something comparable. It's why we're given
tongues and hands for unbuttoning, clasping
and unclasping. It's for doing round-the-world
and putting on the hot mustard yourself.
It's for reaching for the check not fast enough.
There must be an aesthetic not based on death.
There's a small bird called Pure Flame.
There's a tomato called Pride.
There's Duncan, there's Neal, there's me.
There're free matches by the door.

ANOTHER OCEAN

When I saw my friend's daughter,
it healed something in me, when she
held out the string of her duck, said,
Brush. It was a time in my life I couldn't
wear a shirt darker than my pants. I gave up
on the piano entirely, gave up on marriage
and the sub-six-minute mile. It was a time
each hour dazzled like a glass non sequitur
and my handling was inexpert. Hence
these memories like those records they made
after Marley died, dubbed, sugared, the chorus
backing up a pirated ghost. Now when I
put one on, some purist part of me sweeps
from the room but there's still something
sweet in the seams: it's still him, Nesta,
intact, besieged.

One theory of life is all invasion, even
our cells just normalized relations among
hostile industries. Somehow we go on together,
giving each other our acidic, necessary,
pinched-off gifts. Some days the dazzling
dragging its chain. Some days the air chemical
as if the goddess has tired of the color of
her nails. Outside the news stays exploded
in the trees, headline by headline, flashbulbs
of ruin and exclusivity like the glinting waves
of this sea I find myself at. Same ocean Ann
threw herself in after three bottles of Robitussin
and screaming the scream that saved her,
her nightgown phosphorescent as an isotopic ghost.

In a couple days I'll probably look at this
and not see a thing. What affects us most
often is mirage, the rescue ships just vapor
in the heat, the savior's face just rust
on a barn. But right now it seems enough,
like the pictures of the woman in a tub
on the walls of where I write, dull but miraculously
sufficient, something costly about the finish,
as if the photographer spent a lot re-creating
an obsolete technique, an inefficient fixer.
There's such dying out in the world she's
coming to, such smoking down to filters.
But think of her father showing her the sea,
how relieved he is she's not afraid, how
relieved she is it's warm and full of voices.

AESTHETICS

She rummages through her purse, sobbing.
Conventionally sobbing. Her mother had died
but that was long ago. Men shoveling ash
on snow but that was long ago. Not here
by the water, the café where the art
hangs so brutally, organized by size.
Each canvas must have lacked a center until
the nails were driven in. It made her swallow
the piercing. It made her realize her own
misery was part of a larger, more furious
misery she shared with nearly everyone
like breathing in what someone else breathed out.
Now the grass coming off its knees, spring,
the smudge on her bill some remnant of what
arrived at other tables, what she hadn't
wanted. Now the sky euphoric as a new serum.
Once, in of all places a gym, she met a man
whose parachute didn't open. Part of his body
was slightly smaller, smoother, turned slightly
away as if he was half-molted or very slowly
flinching. In the end her mother weighed
nearly nothing so the cremation seemed redundant.
Even with the drugs, the pain showing her
the pit, the tearing into pieces, the searing
places where the canvas shows through
untouched, our part in eternity, molecular,
dispersed. It could be just an emptiness to carry
like a picture of a childhood pet. She remembers
a nun with a pointer in front of a projection
of the cell, naming the organelles and each's
enterprise. The soul was a big black thing. Now
the flowering shrubs release their spermatic dust.

Now the silence option. The long trip option,
driving through the night, stopping just for coffee
and gas, seeing the house so changed, maybe knocking,
maybe being shown in, finding some part still hers.

THE FIRST TIME & THE TIME BEFORE THAT

I'm 17 & she's straddled me
    on her daddy's dentist chair
& the tsunami's about to hit
    the quiet seaside town
        where in the preceding calm
scenes of typical domesticity
    take on a blatant poignancy:
the dog asleep & twitching in the road,
    eggs nestled in egg cartons beside the milk,
        the dentist hosing his hydrangea

until out on the freeway the machine
    that paints the dividing lines
        goes lashingly berserk
& the dentist grabs his gun from the wall
    shouting, My daughter, my practice, my drill

& years later, when she draws a bath,
    instead of water, eyes will gush from the spout,
        my eyes because she said she loved them
because this is how the memory works:
    lyric & monstrous

like Meret Oppenheim's mink cup & saucer.
    I'm bringing the cup to my lips,
        I'm sipping through wet fur
& above me a long purple patch like a glimpse
    of the pure robe & a blank patch
        like a bird opening its wings
            after someone's erased the bird

& I'm 12 & watching the nuns enter the surf
     on their private beach above the bird sanctuary
          in Stone Harbor, New Jersey,
completely shrouded in black bathing habits,
     even black slippers like ballet slippers
& the sea spumes & knocks them joyously down
     & swallows.

Small black swirls within white heaving & green
& already I love Botticelli
     the Birth of Venus that I've seen in a book
          about gods, her left nipple peaking
through the wrist that covers it, *through*
     & drapery sailing away from her crotch

but I love the Metal Men more
     that I'd buy from the blind man's store
handing him a one, saying, This is a one,
     thinking, this is a ten, this is a twenty
          while he feels out the change,
the rack of Batman, Flash, the Human Torch
     beside the tiers of women's licked mouths
          mouthing my name through the brown wrappers,
               sometimes just the orgiastic hair

& in the pages of my comic, the elemental heroes
     stumble & recede, stumble & crest:

Tin flimsy but good in a pinch,
     Iron the strongest, defeated by magnets & rust,
          Mercury useless, inflated with anger,
               Gold brilliant but soft, Lead
                    thuggish, moulding himself into a dome

& Platinum, except for the welds & rivets
     Platinum's female, shining & naked,

best of conductors, last to be made,
        costliest
& in love with her inventor
    who clenches his wrenches each time she approaches—
        how could this happen? he's lost the plans—
who sends them on missions & they always return
    dented, immutable, unalloyed.

ELEGY FOR MY CAT

Toby's dying. Kidney failure. 18 years old,
so the vet and I shrug and nod, each of us
handling her, a ragged ball unsnarling.
She's skinny, been slow on the steps
for weeks, off her food and stinks but
nothing prepared me for this. Just a day ago
she tucked her head into my arm to sleep.
Of course of course of course.

Sometimes starting each next moment
is like turning from one arm-tiring send-off
to another. The yellow streamers. A friend
once asked what I meant by God and I said
God is an event of language, an evocation
of hope that answers itself otherworldly
as an echo but right now that's pure
malarkey just another thought I endure
for its roll and trim
like a ship ice-locked from harbor
signaling with colored flags:
yes, we've got soap and beans aboard,
got a small animal from China
that will sit in your lap
and shit in a box. What I mean by God
is eddies and loss, the whole hollow kit.

Sometimes I'd like to slip
into the dimness ghosts seem to offer
so we don't weep and cower in their passing:
herd in rain shower,
skulls of elephant and vertebra of whale
in sand and less than sand.

The rotating carbon rot of our world.
Adios, sweet cat. Over my head is a shushing
like dirt sifted from a shovel—
the woman upstairs sweeping,
then a quiet stepping away.

THE YEAH, YEAH, YEAH IMPERATIVE

I'm worried how Y carries his money,
dispersed and nondenominational. Worried
that D & L can't stay together, that C & C
can't, that L can't, that J doesn't answer.
So I've come to this place no one goes to
anymore and all the tables are full—the one
N reached across, the one where I hit my head,
the one where B didn't have the keys and
the fact that no one recognizes me clings
like plastic wrap. Dead bugs in each corner
like some previous future: how I dreamed
things might work out: the house with steps
down to the water, the dog retrieving as I fill
my mouth with stones learning to talk to congress.

And to you. Around my face in the bar-length mirror,
the bottles shine orange and cleansed as seraphim,
those attending spirits with no bodies left. Once
in front of The Annunciation, I sobbed like a bride
sailing down the sewer with split fruit, hitched
to a god, a dog, swan, rumor, whoknowswhat. Sometimes
there's no end to sinking, even surrounded
by those clunky wings no human back could flap
and flap is a terrible thing to be left with.
Botticelli cared nothing for musculature.
Botticelli cared nothing for how a fellow
gets out of bed in the morning. I hate
when it feels like we're just stuck

on an elevator or on some island wrecked,
becoming abstractions of some inner state,
upbringing, some occupation as if our thought

was no longer rain but irrigation for a single crop
of artichokes, tobacco or soybeans. Sometimes
I might as well be talking to that sculpture
you made in college and abandoned to the heap,
the one your teacher said showed promise,
the one you always thought of as The Tooth.
I hate that we lose so much, not just each other
but of ourselves so that our parts could be played
by gears with missing cogs, bent nails, bandages.

For instance lately K's been unable to start his day
without "She Loves You," more or less the blasting
yeah, yeah, yeah imperative. For instance what
I did to M. Molecularly, it's the same old thing:
attraction, repulsion a few mad leaps, a dive or two
to lower orbits emitting a hash mark of spectrum
at a time. Some days you burn all purple,
or worse, puce, a color invented out of
desperation like espionage. So it's like
looking through half-drawn blinds all the time,
trying to understand each other, trying
to pick the brown seven out of the whorls
of red eights. Each twilight all interrogation,
each doll in the doll hospital blinked out,
dumbfounded foundling which is how we love
each other, the lady who runs the place saying,
No, the eyes aren't for sale separately.

LEGEND

Someone said lightning from a clear sky
threaded through a house and struck
his picture on its shelf as he died
watching Pele replays on TV
with his wife and bassist. They say
he returned to the hand of Jah like
a severed finger restored.

You've got to imagine a God cutting off
his own finger in the first place.

While Marley finally bowed to radiation
and dismantlement, the girl who taught
me the dance—barely lift the feet, foggy
shrugs and ducks—was in Mauritania,
losing chickens to blight, her hair
to vaccines, losing her help and those
she came to help to a village seer
preaching she was the devil.

When we were young we watched workers
high in girder webs operating spark-spurting
guns, others on the ground with plans,
throwing lifting switches. We thought,
housed there, we'd grow into expertise,
fortify land and seas while clouds amassed
like grateful nations at our knees. We
wanted it called House of Invisible Lion
or House of Hunger Ended and we thought
a giddy smoke-lit dance the start of its
administration. But then the next craze came along,

the next rich costumery, a new beat loud enough
to cover the sound of someone being kicked to death.

Last night I listened to the early, one-track
nearly empty stuff. Wails and taunts
in the empire of wail. In one cut, I swear, bugs
buzz against a screen like the sound of faith
rasping crinkled wings from under a helmet-green
shell. You've got to imagine faith can be caught,

kept living like a thing in a jar,
breath-holes punched in the lid,
a little torn grass in the bottom.

GERMINATIONS

I love sitting here by the screens
as on the porch she tells a friend
how to choose a baby's sex: diet, bath temps,
ways to lie. Outside a torrent wrings
three days' humidity from the air. A few
in plastic ponchos spin by like winning
spinnakers while some relinquish hurry,
give in to new, plastered hairdos,
licked down to a quivering germ of life
like that moment as a child I stood
in a frothed-loose twirl of tree seed
as hail came down and the gutters squirmed.
Now, the unbearable heat broken, awnings
unbloat, locusts crank up their battery-
green volts and I climb the stairs I
heard her climb weeks before we spoke,
late, after she turned each chair upside
down on the swabbed tables in the bar
she worked, after she arrived, the chain guard
tormenting her chain. If I hadn't fixed that
with pliers. If I hadn't rented the rooms
below and my cat died and my friends
in Louisiana said, No, don't come. If she
hadn't turned left then left again. So here
in the clumping dark, my legs knowing
the warped halls, my fingers the light cords,
I'll wait for her to come up from the garden
with cucumbers that have pulsed from seed
free with a bag of Bar-B-Que Fritos,
from an ordinary hole in the ground.

THE LAST THING I REMEMBER

Her sitting by the bed, opening
the envelopes. Late August and hard
to wake with the water lapping nearby
and low sighing. Her sitting

by the bed reading the brief messages
aloud. I can see through her skull
to the flame. The furious congeries
of moths, one flame joining a quiver

of flames. Oh, my maker. Summer and twilight
and warm and a basket of eels from the market.
Hold out your hand, the world's bent,
the ship's masts sinking incrementally

from sight. The machine must be living for me,
all those tubes and stuck-on hookups.
Her opening those colored envelopes,
cousins and friends of friends, sitting

there forever, straightening my fingers.
The cops sweeping their floods above
the corn stubble where I lie, Angles
of incidence. The gemlike splatter,

a smell of burning hair. Even toppled
and crushed, dismembered and strewn,
the statuary seems immense and familiar:
this is the wrist of Hope, this the broken

jaw of Memory. Her pulling my foot
under her dress, between her legs
while we watch in our bar the Cubs
blow the pennant with lousy base running.

Palm trees on her dress. Rain after
a long time of no rain. The marks
on the sidewalks and roads vanishing
in the rain. Behind us there are

these hunkering black shapes
which will swallow us. The continents
roving back to each other, a single forest
covering them, a single glacier. No,

I'm not in pain. I'm in our old house,
watching my mother prune roses,
a ladybug on the screen, two dots.
Pangea. Snow and cypresses. I'm in a boat

and someone's waving from the wharf.
I'm listening to her wringing out
a washrag in the sink, washing her face.
That face. Her opening the envelopes

and having cried enough. I remember absolutely
nothing funny about the road. The curve
then the next curve. Reading those brief
messages. The fog come looking. The mitochondria,

powerhouse of the cell. The Napoleonic Wars,
1802-1815. The Last Supper, the bread torn
and handed out, oh, Lord. I too am
torn. On the wall are marks

as if from passing torches. After
a long while the crowd disperses,
even the eyewitnesses having difficulty
recalling the exact chronology of happenstance.

Chalk marks on the road. The rotating beacons.
I'm standing by a window, over a long drop,
feeling the thick curtain in my hand.
Pop, pop, pop as the curtain rings give.

I'm seeing with more eyes. And falling.
How hard to wake in this big bed
with the chill coming through the cypresses.
Like light, like the back of my hand?

3

ON BEING ASKED BY A STUDENT IF HE SHOULD ASK OUT SOME GIRL

I say get her alone in a kitchen.
I say what Keats said.
I say don't wear that. I display the driftwood
you picked up at McClure's the day we saw the whale.
Part question mark, part claw, part stroke
personified. I say buy her a box of crayons,
the big 64 box. I say you'll be dead soon
anyway. Outside the snow hesitates and thaws
but my office has no windows. I say my office
has no windows and down the hall
the copy machines moan, Again, again,
my chair all swiveling squawk.
I say when I was young.
I tell about carrying your chair across the bridge
and how sick your cockatoo seemed the first weeks
in our new apartment. I say we'll be dead soon
anyway. I explain how after looking half the afternoon
for two socks, one mine, one yours, we find them
under a pillow, nestled together like newts in love.
I say it's hopeless as holding a bag of strawberries
in the rain. I mean what happens to wet paper bags.
I say climb the mountain. I read some Donne aloud
like I'm paid to do. I move the triangle
towards the furnace as indication of the indeterminacy
of all human affairs. There is no triangle, there is no
furnace. I say when I was alone
and miserable. I let the canoe stutter
and drift. I lift my hands like someone asked to dance
a dance I don't know how to. I have this pain.
I have died this way in a previous life,
my armor clattering in the dust.

It's Spring in the Alps. On Venus it's Spring
and tiny Venusians chortle with sobs far beyond
our registers, inventing new forms of love.
I ask her name. I say spell it. I ask, What
did you get on the midterm? Across the hall,
my colleague explains something 18th century
to a cloud of perfume. I am thinking
this morning to discard the opera,
wrote John Cheever in his journal.
To find out why life has this huge dog,
wrote Vallejo in Spanish in Paris.
He fell over coughing up blood.
If I had my notebook, I'd cross everything out.
I love the sea, how it crosses everything out.
I almost start talking about Wisconsin.
I say, You can do two things, maybe three.
I say the final's on Monday,
mostly short answer, some i.d.

SUBSEQUENT COURSE IN TURBULENCE

Some carry baskets of fire on their backs
in hell. Some with snakes under their shirts.
When I had the flu, I dreamed of you again,
the red sweater, shelves of commemorative
thimbles, soap in a milk of decomposition.
Now the streetlights quiver to their first
ineffectual purple throb, more bruise than
illumination. You gotta learn, or at least
that's what Tony's boss said about
a hair on his photo template showing up
as a guidance error on 50 missiles, then
fired him. Not a hair even as crass as
an eyelash, rather part of the body's
golden down.
                    That afternoon I saw you last,
by the sleeping ducks . . . what a mess.
Men in the distance heaved what looked like
orange triangles into the lake. On the radio
candidates admitted defeat, quaking
like my father, overweight, bending over
the car seat. Such grimacing in such simple
acts: backing up a car, sitting on the grass
saying, No, not anymore. Not grass actually,
just stiff rudiment left after scrimmages.
No, not anymore. You know how you feel
when you watch someone cry. I mean really cry,
dredging something from so deep our geological
theories must be revised. We'd like to throw
some sheet over it, this mass brought up
and laid out on the absorptive sawdust,
fizzling, costly, isotopic and crushed.

THE HIVE

All the time asking where are we going,
what sort of dance is this? Of course
it's all about loss, sweet source, honey
that keeps our busted feelers, crimped
limbs, the useless protecting gestures
of our abdomens. No wind really, just
a sense of things not very well secured
like standing on a dock, the tock, tock.
We've all felt that rocking, that loose
rot, something unhappy in the trees
even in our pleased rumple, legs slung
round another, sluiced with the lovely
other at last known, tasted, naked
as a part of speech. Still there's this
going, going. This gone. A woman I love
has this haunted buzz behind her eyes.
A man I love still rides his wrecked bike.
My phone bills, the part in my hair,
my shirt with the cactuses.

*   *   *   *   *   *   *   *   *

I hate what we do to each other.
In the city you can see the people in cardboard boxes.
In the country you can see the pharmaceutical cows.
Upstairs, someone's pounding something together
or pounding it apart. Awake half the night,
plaster everywhere. None of us are to blame,
sitting on the porch, smoking, quitting smoking,
talking about our backs, Italy, finishing
the book on Gertrude Stein, betrayals, talking
about shoes and how we want what everyone wants:
complete devotion and to be left the hell alone.

It all reminds me of Tony's skin.
It all reminds me of Beth misting up whenever
anyone mentions the parrot. It all reminds me
of the woman in Memphis who insulted me
so floridly I felt like I was in love.
While my friend read his poems about Elvis,
she draped her kid over the railing above him.
A sufficient drop and David must have thought
everyone was gasping at his work: the King
shooting TVs—gasp, the King in diapers—gasp.

*   *   *   *   *   *   *   *   *   *   *   *

I know I'm not fooling anyone,
when I say drop dead it means
I fall upon the roses, the traditional
roses. Often just trying to be heard
makes people think you're angry, shaking apart
like a can of screws. Of course
it's all about fear. Last night I watched
a man scream into a pay phone, scream
and whimper and deposit more coins. I've
been him, I've been on the other end
backing off from the uncradled voice
and I've even been the phone, spattered with spit,
close to the furious sea. Didn't they listen
when you told them where you were going?
One day you find yourself unstrung, your stinger
ripped out, inveigled with perfumes. You're standing
on a dock or in a busy field or dragging yourself
through the spilled sugar. Isn't anyone ever going to come?

AMID THESE BLANK MILES

Rain begins all day.
Onto blocks in the lot across the street,
a crane lowers half a house
from a flatbed semi, the open side

sheeted with thick plastic. Someone
must love a house to saw it in half,
pry it from its crimped vasculature,
haul it from Wherever, Arkansas

but how strange it will be to stand
at the same dull sink and watch
a different tree sort the sun's plunder.
Wouldn't a man or a woman feel changed,

even arm hair whorling differently
in suds, even the ring placed on the sill
clutching a different gem and won't it seem,
this single uneventful dusk, like something

within a gem, faceted, dim. One girl
I loved only remains as an early June
afternoon, her saying, This stone is cold,
touching a courtyard bench, a smell

of mowed lawn. Not any of what lathered
over us or the daunting thrall that came
after. How little I've taken with me, I wonder
if I woke tomorrow 200 years ago,

what I'd be. I couldn't explain a light bulb,
battery, even a strike-anywhere match.
No vaccine, no blank filled in on the periodic chart.
Just the same befuddled guy

humming flatly in my tumble. Who
doesn't miss what he's forgotten, dust
on the empty, unruled streets where you swore
were hoofbeats, wheel screech, all manner

of flower and fish, dress with buttons
made of whale teeth, amber, bits of chandelier.
I live in a torn house. Tulips unhinging,
ring-necked geese come and flown. Each morning

I climb down from my lagoon of nothingness.
How carefully impossible to replace
the figurines with always chipped-off feet,
no matter how swaddled in newspaper

and boxed in boxes of styrofoam flakes
and how now the crumpled paper's stories
hold us as never before: rain
throughout the plains; Boston 4, Detroit 0.

THE FINE ARTS

I don't know what Bonnard was up to
but I'm glad he didn't only paint
his wife young as the day he married
or first saw her naked by the earnest
vases, you know love and its retinal
branding iron. Even as she stooped
and sagged, on canvas she's blushed
and ripe in the tub which at first
seems a kind of tribute, of love
but he was probably one quiet hell
to live with; at dinner he might as well
have been talked to by a plate of blue plums.
A fault I know something of:
not seeing someone else in all their
riven unraveling. This print that Lynda
gave me though is of a table and there's
something struggled about its shape,
its uneven red as if he finally fessed up
to age, to death, to his own incapacity
to face any of this in anything but a table.
And throw in all the other sorts of failings
I was going through in that miserable walk-up
where I had it tacked on the wall; a marriage botched,
a nothing job, the women downstairs
controlling the heat, playing the exercise
tape. It was either look at it or
out the window, across a splatter of glass
to the beauty parlor where some nights
at 3, the lights of the tanning booth
would fizz on, purplish as the aura
of someone in big trouble, trying to
remake himself.

Somewhere I've read what Bonnard was after
was how one thing shows through another,
a grief in those spring-drenched rooms,
a loss in parts left undone, harsh
commas of canvas glaring through.
I guess I know what that's about. Last week,
waiting for Alan, who I hadn't seen since
my wife and I got back together, I
could feel the dusk gilding everything
and yet these moments seem simultaneously
extinguished like torches plunged in waves.
She was marking a postcard with an X
for where we were, lovely in the new maroon
and black jacket we had bought that day
after looking at Chagall lithographs,
thankful finally my credit card doesn't go
to 5,000 because we'd have the chalky
blue one now, the wading, wadded lovers
with the mule and no way to pay for it.
Waiting there, that restored, the waitress
coming with our beers, I kept finding myself
refreshing some loss, going back to
that walk-up. Everything seemed fraught
with its own diminishment and desertion,
rainbowed: it's raining and the sun is out.

Now I've hung up Chagall's Time Is a River
of Forgetting, where a fish is a parrot's wing.
From the parrot's beak a hand, from the hand
a violin, from the violin a march played
in a way to make you cry, make you put your head
on a table beneath a picture of a table
which is only the memory of a table. Wobble,
wobble, everything wobbling like a newborn horse,
like a boy leading the horse from the burning barn,

his arm where he holds the mane connected
to the fire, its insistent throb. Somehow
he knows to throw his pajama top over
the horse's eyes as if he was prepared for this,
waiting, as if he had lived it all before
and knew, as he walked toward the car lights,
he'd only to move from one brilliance to the next.

STRIP/RUIN
(DeKOONING WOMAN)

What with the men shouting and pounding.
A three-color projection wheel
in front of a single flood. First off
blue as if submerged and who can breathe?
The spigot opening and the money involved.
What isn't a stitch of glimpses?
First the gloves and then the sleeves.
Not the red yet. Not the incineration.
Not the mouth yet.
The men sit there as she dances yellow,
the stage risen above the percussive pit.
Smoking while she entices the nothing
she's closed her eyes for.
Become become become.
Augmented by ferocity and longing
like a gear in the stomach.
A man has to eat.
Touching the ceiling like it has spawned her
and she wants recalled. You asked
and they brought you the bottle.
Her touching the ceiling by now nearly naked.
Some things we love for their difficulty.
The recovery of great ruins.
The plow that has so much to do with the finding.
The pieces pried from the tilled mud.
Beauty yanked up like a radish.
The pain involved.
Fine bits of lace and bells and tattoos
and the light by now red. Red spreading.
Red falling over. Red propped up.

The connivance and sugars and arm utterly bent
to accomplish the last position.
The mouth, the mouth now everywhere.

KITES & MASKS

What if they hadn't begun with loss,
there amid the piles of oyster shells,
the shucked carapaces of crawfish, lemons
misted dry, the spices stinging the skin's
miniscule splits, glutter and glister, sweet
feeding, sucking out, sweet, sweet, a third-beer

blearyness softening even the Cornhuskers
braying at the bar, the big game tomorrow,
erupting spores of cologne. We love
the lovers, the way she slips her heel
in and out of her shoe, him telling
about chasing the sheet music, Mozart,

complete belief in the tongue in the ear,
hand on the breast, all the nerves opening
their mouths, I do I do, but we know
what's coming too, the man on his face
in the sawdust, the woman in a slip accusing
the mirror, the set-out dish of milk dried,

caked, faceted with ants. So they lead each other
back to the hotel with its paper electronic
keys, her with the pearls, him the gold scissors
shaped like an ibis, its beak the blades,
and the scarves that cost nearly nothing
by the wharf. Was there any other way to begin?

Silk, my love, seeing through silk. The brief
squalls force everyone under awnings, together
into archways. In a window, a slow-motion
smear of desire, struck and bluish, two

strippers want rid of something glittering
between their legs. Do what you want

with their cries as the crowd turns the corner
to the cemetery and suddenly song seems
sufficient, all the flowers making sense,
each a blaze, lips in blaze, tongues on fire,
"Come closer, closer, lie down.
How do you like to be touched?"

LIKE SADNESS IN MUSIC

I have to lie on the floor
so the screams from downstairs
precipitate into words but even that
is no help. Like salts. Because they stung
I thought salts somehow good for wounds.
Sometimes I watch her dog, circular in the yard.
A gate, an outer gate, two locks more,
there are too many keys.
I remember writing at my school desk,
under the cloud of the correct, my pencil
slipping into dents, tracing others' curses,
declarations and codes. Others, others, others.
Like rain. Like rain filling a crack
then ice cracking it further.
But I can't imagine what to press so hard
about. What quotient? What crush?
I know so little I'm kept awake by silences,
by rests. Whole notes of silence among the silent pines.
It's difficult to guess what anyone wants and my glasses
steam when I come back inside. Years later
I mean. In a different state.
I only intended to be gone a moment.
Just some air.
I don't mean to give the impression I'm alone
but sometimes kneeling by the radiator
isn't enough, the hole in the floor
where the pipes and light come through.
Like sadness in music.
Like elucidation.
Like the men humped over the cello
in the cam of some combusted grunt
that comes out woeful and woefuller.

Nothing fits.
I remember following the trigonometry on the board,
how it seemed we were all on the tip of some tangent
that could be understood, every dream confined to a wave,
every desire a cosine. But there was Lucy
in front of me. It wasn't a leg thing.
It wasn't a breast thing.
It was a back-of-the-head thing.
A small-white-dog-in-the-rain thing.
February and tangerines.
Erasing, erasing, not saying a word.

AFTER 8 BEERS, I RISE INTO THE TURBULENCE

Pittsburgh airport, early winter, my plane
socked in and the first two beers, 2.50 per,
I try to drink slow. The receipts tag the clock
precisely: 7:54, 8:18 so I could be sipping

time itself, lapping all the numbing events
puddled in the news like a shade in Hell
guzzling goat's blood. Down the hatch
to John Lennon shot, gulp goes the baby stuck

in the storm pipe, swallow hard for all those
hostages going down sideways. On TV a blizzard too,
two teams skate furiously one red, one black
like warring ants, the puck obscured in the down-

and up- and overpour so there's nothing
to connect the surge and combat to except
the idea of a puck which always comes too late.
8:38. I've not nearly had enough and

the guy next to me, also stuck, piling up
a thicket of plastic swords, shows me a picture
in one of the flesh magazines you have to reach
way back for: the girl in a froth

of stuffed animals, shucked, clutching a giraffe.
My daughter, he says although I don't believe him.
The expression on her face is not a look a father
should ever see, step or otherwise. And his face?

Maybe he's already turned to stone, maybe
he's spat out as much as he can and flies
from runway bar to runway bar like a man
trapped in an early Twilight Zone, hunting

for someone to set him free, unburden him,
someone who'll say Oh yeah, this is my son
on page 23, my wife on the trapeze, here's Mom
on the leash. Maybe I'm as dead as my Dad,

maybe my plane's already crashed and what
we're dealing with is a bunch of ghosts
trying to wash out the last gristle of their
earthly lives, what's stopping us from rising

in an ectoplasmic burn-off. He probably didn't
believe me either when I said I was going
from one funeral to another, that last bit
just to keep things lively. But it was snowing

too hard to be Hell and the music told us
we'd better not cry and I just swallowed,
didn't say much more, just fluttered his magazine,
recognized no one, read the columns about

people having sex in grocery stores, tollbooths,
airplane washrooms, places you'd think utterly
incommodious, hostile to whatever it is
we work so hard to give and take from and to each other.

4

ROTHKO'S YELLOW

What I don't understand is the beauty.
The last attempts of the rain, my shoulders
aching from all afternoon with the ladders
and the hour with her. I watch the rainbow
until I have to focus so hard I seem
to create it. Thinking of her watching
this storm, wanting him. This lightning.
This glut in the gutters. Now only
the yellow left. Now the blue
seeped out. The purple gone. The red
gone. People downstairs playing Bach,
the quiet attenuated Bach. She must
have tried and tried. The holes drilled in.
The small man in the movie who looked
like laughter would kill him. The carnation
farmer who left snared birds for the woman
he loved. Who would hang himself after
stitching her ribbon to his chest,
What I don't understand is the beauty.
I remember the theatre in Berkeley where
we sat eating cucumbers, watching the colossal
faces played over with colossal loss.
I would get off early and meet her outside,
her hair always wet. All last night
I listened to the students walk by until 3,
only the drunk left, the rebuffed and
suddenly coupled. What did I almost
write down on the pad by my bed
that somehow lowered me into sleep? One morning
when she and I still lived together,
the pad said only, cotton. Cotton.
Sometimes it's horrible, the things said

outright. But nothing explains the beauty,
not weeping and shivering on that stone bench,
not kneeling by the basement drain.
Not remembering otherwise, that scarf she wore,
the early snow, her opening the door
in the bathing light. She must have tried
and tried. What I don't understand is the beauty.

TRANSUBSTANTIATION

Once I found six letters,
explicit letters. Once I went through
a windshield. Sometimes it's enough just
to talk to each other and we'll never
be the same but why else do we sit here,
telling even the worst of our lives
with such goofy looks, stirring
the whipped cream in. One morning
you go to her studio and there's an angel.
One morning you go and there's a black oval
with wrings but that too must be part of it,
the hectoring and hankering after, flux
in a thicket, the spirit throwing off
its rags, stringing the bow. Sometimes
you think one thing but it comes out
another, think you're saying potato
and they bring you a basket of nails
but what delicate gold nails.
Such a brilliant morning, we mistook
the roofers on the hill for flames.
Once in Italy, slithering squid guts
out with the flat of the knife
I felt another life pass through me
with a whiff of kerosene. Once
when I carried my father. Once
when I came out from under anesthetic
with someone beside me laboring at
new vowels and now, my dear, what
are those things on your scarf? Flamingos,
Irises? The kimonos of the lovers
on the Bridge of Sighs? Oh, it's like
a magic trick where we're hooded with

gunnysacks and beaten with blackjacks
yet we emerge intact, just flushed
from breathing in a bag. Emerging: the stone
rolled back, Michelangelo's slaves, calling
the dog at dusk, all of us beguiled, chagrined,
nearly sick with rich disclosure.

OTHER OBIT

Night, what more do you want?
Why this second-per-second scream?
My friend Nick used to sit all night
in the same booth all night
with a pile of quarters for pinball
and jukebox. He loved the one where
the balls disappeared up the bonus-lit chute.
He loved the song where the wife smelled shirts,
all tilt and jilt and sometimes he'd bring back
a waitress who'd play the records we never
played. You know the ones, everyone has
those records. It was almost the age
of Aquarius and once we wanted to remember
the comedy, movies, the primitive flutes.
I'd come down and there they'd be, nearly
glamorous with smoke and wine, all the shades
pulled. Night, even then you couldn't give up,
there was your lariat in the corner,
your ashes everywhere. It might have been
the drugs we kept zip-locked in the cranial
cavity of a pig, a skull Nick found where
a pig had died or at least a pig's head had died.
Aren't I cute? Don't you like my legs? Night,
what pleases you? From the beginning,
the body's full of holes. Night, these are the facts
and the philosophy of facts. See how they
grin back fast faces like the 23 windows
he fell past. Jumped past. When does a jump
become a fall? There were a few more floors
but 23 was enough, enough climbing he must have
thought and then opened the window by the stairs.
I thought at least there'd be a note.

Help or a simple declarative sentence.
They seemed to take forever with the organ,
the hothouse arrangements and how his parents
hated me that open-hole day.
Adios, au revoir, good night. You want me
on my knees? I'm on my knees. When I was a child,
When I was a cantaloupe. When I was
an enemy spacecraft hovering over the Pentagon.
Tick tock and such a puddle. Tick tock
my soul to keep. Tick tock and such
deep wagons on so many panged wheels.

WHAT TO CALL IT

We met in a bar, et cetera. Then
one afternoon—she must have worked
all day tearing the bits of paper square,
tugging out and rolling the tape, even serifs
on the tiny letters—when I came home
everything had its name, chair said chair,
wall wall and each word shook
as if cut from bolts of gauze,
as if purified by scream.
There was that rocky surge
like boats leaving harbor, those
twittering, yellow streamers.
Good-bye, good-bye I almost waved
chilled by fast evaporation.
Later the hospital gave her her own tag,
quelling, mewing, the job done at last,
and kept her. I can't say it was love,
the way we tore at each other,
upsetting the wine, a spreading puddle
we called rose, no, Africa, no,
a woman in a hat. Our configurations:
the girl turning hag, the man's face
made entirely of sprawled genitalia
you can't stop seeing once you do.
I've read that words are just metaphors
gone old-bone brittle. Nothing out there
for "leaf" spangling in our heads, nothing
without singular dots of rot and yet,
like callous and chain link fences,
these words somehow protect us.
It was autumn, the air turned ciderish,
the orchard fugued with red and brown,

bee-yammer and rustle-down.
This is not about love although there I was
without love, my hands at ten and two on the wheel.
Gentleness seemed required getting her
into the car. Force seemed required
and later formality on the street.

STORMS

I've been sweating again, a symptom
so far only of itself just as those stray
explosions belong to no holiday,
no larger sequence of battle. Years ago
in another house, I'd wake like this
and stalk the other rooms, naked and
monstrously alive as if a thousand ears
had sprung from my skin. Sometimes
back in bed, a woman would be sobbing hard,
hiccuping, so I'd get a glass of water
that would harp the walls, get the pills
from her purse, stroke her until they worked.
Other nights she'd be waiting,
wetting herself with her hand and rapidly
we'd fuck, panting like harnessed dogs
who didn't know miles ago their master
had frozen in the sled. Stop? No one
can stop. It starts out Wednesday then
it's Tuesday and you're sitting with A
in a café under some ornamental masks.
She's disturbed. You're disturbed.
A whole cloudburst of disturbance.
Inside the purple mask, there're more feathers,
each with a quill directed inward, against
the face. Awful to be in it as well as
outside of it, hooting with fear. Will A
stay with B and is B's cancer-ruddled mother
choosing this moment to die, can anyone
actually choose a moment to die, choose
to die at all and what is a moment anyway
but a thing made entirely of its own vanishing?
It all gets complex fast. You're just

sitting there, nodding, then BOOM, the temple's
in ruins and the emperor has you up at dawn
beating the ocean with chains. I wonder
if C will ever forgive me and will D ever
pick up his phone? Then the dream of the sun.
Then the dream of the black dogs and
saying yes in the desert. There were those
masks on the terrified wall. Maybe she should go.
Maybe I should explain. When the fire next door
is out, the firemen loiter and smoke in the rain.
Who hasn't wanted to be a fireman
in a rubber raincoat, everything ash and hissing?
In the rain she decided to leave him
and in the rain she decided to go back.
Such friendships and fires. Such lies
and masks and love. I've only myself to blame.
In the rain we were singing. In the rain
I am empty, I am stuck. In the rain
I am pilfering and wanton and struck.

MARRIAGE

Most of us remember finding our first
nest. The delightful knitting and knotting
of hair and twigs and cellophane. Mud
and paper, comfort and down. Simultaneously
we admire its strength and fragility
like that day outside the store, unable
to leave each other even though we agreed.

After you said what you wanted.
After I said what I wanted.

Inside the window, the dismantled mannequins
were way ahead of us on spring. Sometimes,
in storms, a door bursts open and in come
the sloppy hostile sergeants of air
and even our confessions won't stop the ransacking.
Or sometimes a deck chair tips over as if someone
has risen from it swiftly, having seen
something out there tangled in the strings
he'd long ago thought he'd cut. Out there
where there's nothing now, just the trees
upholding their intentions, the road where
a truck carries by the names of fruit.

Things fall down in the wind. Sometimes
that's all they have in common
like two people who meet on a hospital elevator.
Even though they know what's coming,
how the doors will open on all that beige
chosen for the pain it can absorb, maybe
they'll find a moment away from all this, alone,
some wine, sunset, propellers.

Sometimes it seems like a lesson in all we've
nearly lost, by turns humbling and invigorating,
like pinching out candles with a licked
finger and thumb. It's not always darkness
we fall through but it's always earth
where we land: spring and sprouts,
the welts beneath where your suit fits snug
which make you seem more naked. Everyone
remembers crumbling that first nest when
even the fallen chicks, bald, brainless,
crepuscular, even death didn't faze us.
But now we remember mother dragging box
after box to the curb. We remember
a man weeping with pearls slung
between his hands. We remember the woman
who couldn't resist and became so sorry.
It isn't just a matter of standing on the porch
listening for the inklings of the stars. It isn't
just lifting her dress. It's carrying something,
a cup too full, a phone number, a thought like
a letter torn then taped together again.

THE SOUL

Because all afternoon we watch vultures
and Michael says if he had health
he'd like to hunt, not for the kill
but the long stalk, the hunched wait
in the weeds and because the arm, limp
in his lap as a fish in a sleeve,
still scoops up warmth and touch and pain.
Because for me whole years remain
only as scatters of walkway stone,
linoleum step-dimmed by the stove, the sink,
the back way out with its screen door unhinged
and if you asked, I would have sworn, yes,
I love her. Not the clawing but the pinioned
shadow crossing the dry gold hills.
Not Christ nailed but brought down,
the tenderness of two summoned women,
each taking a blood-cold foot, road grit
passing from heel to hand, the immense quiet
and weight of quiet, even the guard
careful to keep cloth over the side-slung
genitals. All without acrimony or remorse
yet warped with hope as starlight
because even starlight comes cloaked
with aberration, the blue throttle
of receding, the red hurtling
forth. Because our very looking creates,
inseparable from the looked-at, atom
of atom: quark, scent, hue, the minute
engine within each engine, each bowl of fire.
Because we know we will never know, not
from fingering the wounds, not from calculation,
ephemerides or lens. Not the clawing

but the shadow. No crown or flower, only
sepal, thorn, the withering bulk and nodding,
our momentary gentle attendance as someone calls,
come look at the moon, come watch the waves.

About the Author

DEAN YOUNG has published five books of poems, *Skid* (2002), *First Course in Turbulence* (1999), *Strike Anywhere* (1995) which won the first Colorado Poetry Prize, *Beloved Infidel* (1992) and *Design With X* (1988). A recipient of a Stegner fellowship from Stanford University, two fellowships from the National Endowment for the Arts and one from the Provincetown Fine Arts Work Center, in 2002 he was awarded a Guggenheim Fellowship. Young is on the permanent faculty of the Iowa Writers' Workshop and also teaches in the Warren Wilson low residency MFA program. He splits his time between Iowa City and Berkeley where he lives with his wife, the novelist Cornelia Nixon and his Abyssinian, Keats.

"A beautifully written, brilliant, deeply philosophical novel."
— **Chuck Kinder**

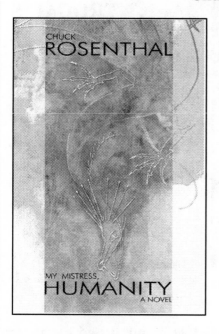

MY MISTRESS, HUMANITY
A Novel
by CHUCK ROSENTHAL

ISBN 0-9676003-5-9
$17.95 Softcover

Not far in the future a series of catastrophic weather events have crippled the technological infrastructure of the world and humankind is on the verge of total annihilation. One man knows the secret and only one young woman can save the planet. From Chuck Rosenthal comes an apocalyptic vision of the future, *My Mistress, Humanity*. Rosenthal's gothic vision of the future is both terrifying and beautiful. In the gorgeous lyric prose for which he's known, like the creator of a modern-day Frankenstein, Rosenthal takes us on a journey towards humanity's ultimate destruction and redemption.

Hollyridge Press

"There's hopped-up frenzy and plenty of wit here."
— **Kirkus Reviews**

JACK KEROUAC'S AVATAR ANGEL
His Last Novel
by CHUCK ROSENTHAL

ISBN 0-9676003-2-4
$23.95 Hardcover

Chuck Rosenthal discovers a lost, unpublished manuscript from the King of the Beats—Jack Kerouac—who returns from the grave to set off one last time, charting chart the experience and conscience of a generation grappling with a changed culture. At once visionary and elegant, restless and incantatory, Rosenthal's writing achieves a rare beauty, his sensitivity to language as great as Kerouac's. In an exuberant novel of great wit and great loss, the emptiness Kerouac encounters in this final journey is palpable and tragic, unforeseen but inevitable, both familiar and foreign to America's most famous mystic traveler.

Hollyridge Press

"You will be dazzled and amazed."
— **David St. John**

THE LOVE-TALKERS
An Erotic Fable
by GAIL WRONSKY

ISBN 0-9676003-3-2
$23.95 Hardcover

The beauty of Gail Wronsky's poetic language has never been better displayed than in *The Love-talkers*. Mexico City, with its parks and cathedrals provides a lush backdrop for the story. A sumptuously rendered book, celebrating passionate imagination with all the sublime joy of physical love, Wronsky's elegiac style summons up the magic of Latin American fiction in this novel of desire which brings us into the depths of erotic charge. From ecstatic awakenings to feverish enactments of appetite, Wronsky's novel reveals what happens when we find our deepest yearnings made true.

Hollyridge Press

"An amazing use of language and clarity of description compels the reader on."
—**Patricia Gulian**, *Book/Mark*

HUNGER
and Other Stories
by Ian Randall Wilson

ISBN 0-9676003-0-8
$12.95 Paperback

In his first collection of short stories, Ian Randall Wilson's characters are driven by intense yearnings for the satisfaction of their most basic human desires. All are thwarted by personal shortcomings, or the shortcomings of others, in their attempts to fulfill their longing. Here are 14 stories which "despite their restlessness," former *North American Review* editor Robley Wilson says, "glitter with persistent hopes."

Hollyridge Press

"Alexander is an accomplished writer with a deft hand for characterization."
— **Hillary Johnson**, *LA Weekly*

THE FINAL AUDIT
and Other Stories
by Ronald Alexander

ISBN 0-9676003-1-6
$12.95 Paperback

In Ronald Alexander's debut novel, Dexter Giles lives a double life, balancing a straight-jacketed career in the homophobic towers of corporate culture with his secret world as a gay man. Nancy Lamb writes, "The interconnected stories in this novel are serious and unforgettable and told with humor and insight. Alexander displays an intuitive grasp of the complexity of family relationships and the power of long-term friendships."

Hollyridge Press

"Among the new magazines. . .one of the best has to be *88*."
—*Literary Magazine Review*

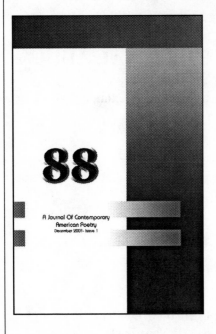

88
A Journal of Contemporary
American Poetry (Issue 1)
Denise L. Stevens (editor)

ISBN 0-9676003-4-0
$13.95 Paperback

Issue 1 features an amazing range of poetry:
—The wonderfully comic sensibilities of Amiri Baraka: "I get horrible letters / From Ghosts / Demanding / Money."
—Dean Young writes in an echo of the New York School: "I don't ask for much: a little cleavage, / the honey of deconstruction to go along / with my cereal but something's scorched / my curtsey, one of my eyes's funny."
—Roger Weingarten's poignant narrative poem about fathers: "Into the no man's land / behind the flimsy curtain of my / resolve not to let them / get to me."
—Postmodernism from Gail Wronsky: "She's // greasy as a melancholy rhyme. What / self-esteems are   each day, paradoxically, / dismantled in her beehive?"
Plus essays and reviews. . .

www.hollyridgepress.com

THE BEST IN AMERICAN POETRY!

88

A Journal of Contemporary
American Poetry (Issue 2)
Ian Randall Wilson (editor)

ISBN 0-9676003-6-7
$13.95 Paperback

Including the work of:

Barry Ballard	Jim Barnes	Bill Berkson
Killarney Clary	Patricia Corbus	Stephen Corey
Stuart Dischell	Richard Garcia	Reginald Gibbons
Joy Gladding	Elton Glaser	Rachel Hadas
Jonathan Holden	Mark Jarman	Kate Knapp Johnson
Peter Johnson	Carolyn Lei-lanilau	Gerald Locklin
Fred Moramarco	Elisabeth Murawski	Mary Ruefle
Ron Silliman	Alan Sondheim	Terese Svoboda
James Tate	Elaine Terranova	Susan Wheeler
Charles Harper Webb	Eve Wood	Gail Wronsky

Plus reviews. . .

Hollyridge Press

"A welcome addition to the literary world."
—*www.newpages.com*

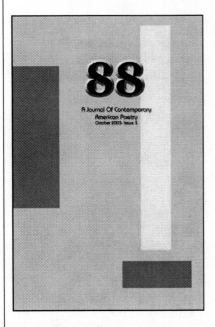

88

A Journal of Contemporary
American Poetry (Issue 3)
Ian Randall Wilson (editor)

ISBN 0-9676003-7-5
$13.95 Paperback

Including the work of:

Joan Aleshire	Pamela Alexander	Dick Allen
Dorothy Barresi	Jeanne Marie Beaumont	Cal Bedient
Anselm Berrigan	Michael C. Blumenthal	Ralph Burns
Tom Clark	Tenaya Darlington	James Doyle
kari edwards	Roger Fanning	Chris Forhan
Mark Halperin	Daniel Halpern	Matthea Harvey
William Heyen	Tony Hoagland	Patricia Spears Jones
Richard Jones	Peter Levitt	Gerald Locklin
Thomas Lux	Elisabeth Murawski	David Wagoner
Rosmarie Waldrop	Eleanor Wilner	Gail Wronsky

Plus essays and reviews. . .

www.hollyridgepress.com